5/15

Autism

BY MICHELLE LEVINE

amicus
high interest

Amicus High Interest is an imprint of Amicus
P.O. Box 1329, Mankato, MN 56002
www.amicuspublishing.us

Library of Congress Cataloging-in-Publication Data
Levine, Michelle, author.
 Autism / by Michelle Levine.
     pages cm. — (Living with ...)
 Summary: "Describes what it is like to live with autism, what its
symptoms are, and how it is treated"— Provided by publisher.
 Audience: K to grade 3.
 Includes bibliographical references and index.
 ISBN 978-1-60753-479-2 (library binding) —
 ISBN 978-1-60753-692-5 (ebook)
 1. Autism—Juvenile literature. 2. Autism—Treatment—Juvenile
literature. I. Title. II. Title: Living with ... autism.
 RC553.A88L485 2015
 616.85'882—dc23

                                        2013032381

Editors: Kristina Ericksen and Rebecca Glaser
Series Designer: Kathleen Petelinsek
Book Designer: Heather Dreisbach
Photo Researcher: Kurtis Kinneman

Photo Credits: dbimages/Alamy, cover; Linda Epstein/Getty
Images, 5; Adrian Sherratt/Alamy, 6; Lou McGill/Alamy, 9;
David White/Alamy, 11; Nir Alon/Alamy, 12; ZUMA Press,
Inc./Alamy, 15; Robin Nelson/ZUMA Press/Corbis, 17;
Jodi Cobb/National Geographic Society/Corbis, 19; WU
HONG/epa/Corbis, 20; PETER KOMKA/epa/Corbis, 23;
Jeff Greenberg/Alamy, 24; Daily Mail/Rex/Alamy, 27; Rob
Crandall/Alamy, 28

Printed in the United States of America at Corporate Graphics
in North Mankato, Minnesota.

10 9 8 7 6 5 4 3

Table of Contents

What Is Autism?

Do you ever like being alone? This boy does. Speaking is hard for him. So is listening to others. He doesn't like looking people in the eye. And being with kids his age is hard. He loves his mom, dad, and sister. But he mostly likes being by himself. He has **autism**. Its full name is **autism spectrum disorder**, or ASD.

Children with autism often prefer to be alone.

Some kids with ASD use picture cards. This helps them tell how they feel.

I want a red bike

I hear tambourine + and drum

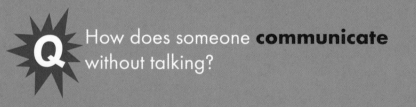

Q How does someone **communicate** without talking?

ASD is different for everyone. But it affects people in similar ways. One way is talking. Some kids with ASD cannot talk at all. Other kids can talk. But they have trouble with words. Expressing their thoughts and feelings is hard. Others with ASD are good speakers. But they may talk too loudly. Or their voices may sound strange.

Some people with ASD use picture cards. They also use **gestures**. There are many ways to "talk" without using words.

Making friends is also hard for kids with ASD. They may not like what other kids like. They have their own interests. It might be frogs, computers, or airplanes. Often, they talk about their interests a lot. They don't notice when someone gets bored. They don't understand when others are sad, mad, or happy. And they have a hard time listening.

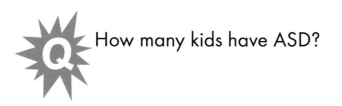 How many kids have ASD?

Children with ASD see things differently.

 One out of every 88 kids in the United States has ASD. Many of them are boys. But girls can have ASD too.

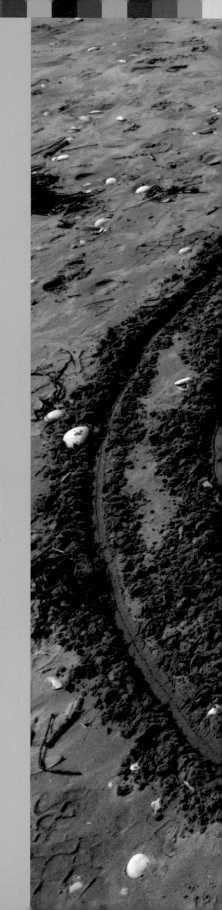

Repeating things is another **symptom** of ASD. Kids with ASD often do the same thing over and over. It could be flapping their arms. It could be twirling around. It could be lining up toys or playing with string. Doing the same thing feels good. It makes kids with ASD feel calm.

A boy draws circles in the sand. It makes him feel calm.

This boy cannot talk very well.
A health care worker uses toys
to help him.

Q Do grown-ups get ASD?

What Causes ASD?

Why do some kids have ASD? Doctors are not sure. But they are learning more about it. ASD is not **contagious**. You can't catch it like a cold. Many kids are born with it. They may act differently as babies. Other kids show signs of ASD later. The ASD symptoms show up at age two or three.

 No. ASD begins in childhood. But it lasts a person's whole life.

Doctors know that ASD starts with the brain. The brain is very important. It controls how we think, move, and feel. The brains of kids with ASD work differently. That can make some things hard for them. But it can make other things easy. Some kids with ASD can remember many facts. Others are good at music, art, or math.

This girl has ASD. She is very good at playing the piano.

Some people need extra help to get dressed.

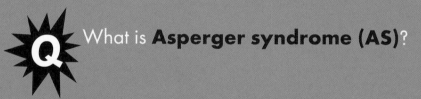
Q What is **Asperger syndrome (AS)?**

Types of ASD

Everyone is different. No two people are the same. That's true of kids with ASD too. Some have **severe** ASD. They never learn to speak. They have trouble doing simple things. Getting dressed is hard. They may have trouble eating with a fork or brushing their teeth. They need a lot of help each day.

AS is a mild type of ASD. Kids with AS can do most things. But making friends is still hard.

Other kids have less severe ASD. They can do a lot themselves. But talking is hard. They may not understand how to share and take turns. They don't make friends easily. Often, they would rather be alone.

Some kids with ASD have no trouble talking. They are good at many things. But they have trouble belonging. Taking time to get to know them helps a lot.

These boys are twins. But each one has a different form of ASD.

Treating ASD

ASD has no cure. But a person with ASD can improve many skills. It starts with a team of helpers. The team includes doctors and other health care workers. It includes teachers, too.

Kids with ASD have to work extra hard to learn social skills. They practice speaking, listening, and making friends.

Kids with ASD can learn to play together.

Some kids with ASD seem clumsy. They have trouble controlling their bodies. Using their hands is also hard. Health care workers help build a person's strength and balance.

Certain senses may also be a problem. Loud sounds upset some kids with ASD. So do new foods. The health care team helps with that, too.

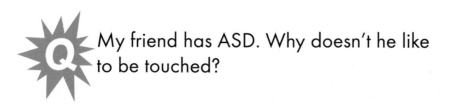
My friend has ASD. Why doesn't he like to be touched?

This girl practices holding a pen to write.

 Some kids with ASD have a strong sense of touch. Even a gentle touch feels bad. It is important to respect their feelings.

Children and teens with AS can go to special camps for fun.

Q My brother has ASD. Why does he get so angry sometimes?

Living with ASD

Kids with ASD like **routines**. They like the same schedule. They like the same meals. Sudden change is upsetting. Parents and teachers try to respect the routines.

Some kids with ASD go to a special school. There they learn new skills. Others go to a regular school. But they may need extra help.

Having ASD can be hard. It can make a person feel worried, sad, or scared. Find out what is making your brother angry. Help him solve his problems.

What about adults with ASD? Some need a lot of help. Simple tasks will always be hard for them. Others may always feel a little different. But they can lead successful lives. Some are scientists, artists, musicians, and more. They have friends and jobs.

Kids with ASD can become happy adults. This man is an artist.

This boy might need time alone.
But he also needs friends!

Do you have a friend with ASD? Ask him about his interests. Find things you both like to do. Be patient. Help him solve problems. And give him time alone when he needs it. Most of all, be a good friend. Then everyone can get along!

Glossary

Asperger syndrome (AS) A mild form of ASD.

autism A health condition of the brain that affects how a person speaks, feels, and acts.

autism spectrum disorder (ASD) The full name for autism.

communicate To get across thoughts and feelings through words, body movements, or pictures.

contagious An illness that is spread from person to person.

gestures Body movements that express thoughts, feelings, or needs.

routine A schedule or set of activities that is the same each day.

severe Serious or extreme.

symptom Something caused by an illness or health problem.

Read More

Amenta, Charles A. *Russell's World: A Story for Kids about Autism.* Washington, D.C.: Magination Press, 2011.

Tourville, Amanda Doering. *My Friend Has Autism.* Mankato, Minn.: Picture Window Books, 2010.

Veenendall, Jennifer. *Why Does Izzy Cover Her Ears?* Shawnee Mission: Autism Asperger Publications, 2009.

Websites

CDC Kid's Quest—Autism
www.cdc.gov/ncbddd/kids/autism.html

Kid's Health—Autism
kidshealth.org/kid/health_problems/brain/autism.html

Neuroscience For Kids—Autism
faculty.washington.edu/chudler/aut.html

Index

About the Author

Michelle Levine has written and edited many nonfiction books for children. She loves learning about new things—like ASD—and sharing what she's learned with her readers. She lives in St. Paul, Minnesota.